Happy Birthday Lee
Love from:
Aunty Doreen, Uncle Harold
-1979-   Ian & Joanne.
AF504079

First published in Great Britain 1979 by Ward Lock
Limited, 116 Baker Street, London, W1M 2BB,
a member of the Pentos Group.

© **Grisewood & Dempsey Limited 1978.**

Designed and produced by Grisewood & Dempsey
Limited, Grosvenor House, 141–143 Drury Lane,
London, WC2B 5TG.

All rights reserved. No part of this publication may be
reproduced, stored in a retrieval system, or transmitted in
any form or by any means, electronic, mechanical,
photocopying, recording, or otherwise, without the
permission of the Copyright owner(s).

Printed in Italy by Vallardi Industrie Grafiche, Milan

BRITISH LIBRARY CATALOGUING IN PUBLICATION
DATA
Chinery, Michael
 Pictorial atlas of animals
 1. Zoogeography – Juvenile literature
 I. Title
 591.9   QL101

ISBN 0-7063-5668-3

Ward Lock's
Pictorial Atlas of Animals

BY MICHAEL CHINERY

Editor
Abigail Frost

Illustrators

Graham Allen
Mike Atkinson
Trevor Boyer
Tim Bramfitt

Chris King
Robert Morton
David Pickard
Clive Spong

Ward Lock Limited · London

Contents

Animals of the World

Perhaps the most important thing for any animal is the place it lives in. For this is what rules the sort of food it can find, the sort of home it can build, and even the size and shape of its body. Down the centuries, animals have evolved with adaptations to live comfortably in almost any conditions. In the deserts, there are animals which can live without drinking. In the polar regions, there are animals which can find plants to eat even when the ground is covered with snow.

If there is a gap to be filled – a way of building a home, or a kind of food to be eaten – an animal is sure to fill it. Think of the way birds have learned to live in towns – building nests in the walls and eaves of houses, and feeding partly on rubbish – and you will see that this is true. This has happened in a very short time, compared with the history of the Earth. But exactly the same thing has been happening for thousands of centuries. Slowly the Earth's climate has changed, continents have moved apart, and animals have had to adapt to new ways of life. Over a very long time, their bodies have changed too.

Usually the animals which fill a particular gap in different continents are quite like one another. Sometimes they are even the same species, their ancestors having scattered before the continents finally parted. This is why we find many of the same animals in Europe and North America. But sometimes, through an accident of evolution, they are very different. The antelopes and the kangaroos do not appear to be very alike. But both fill the same gap – grazing on the vast plains – in Africa and in Australia.

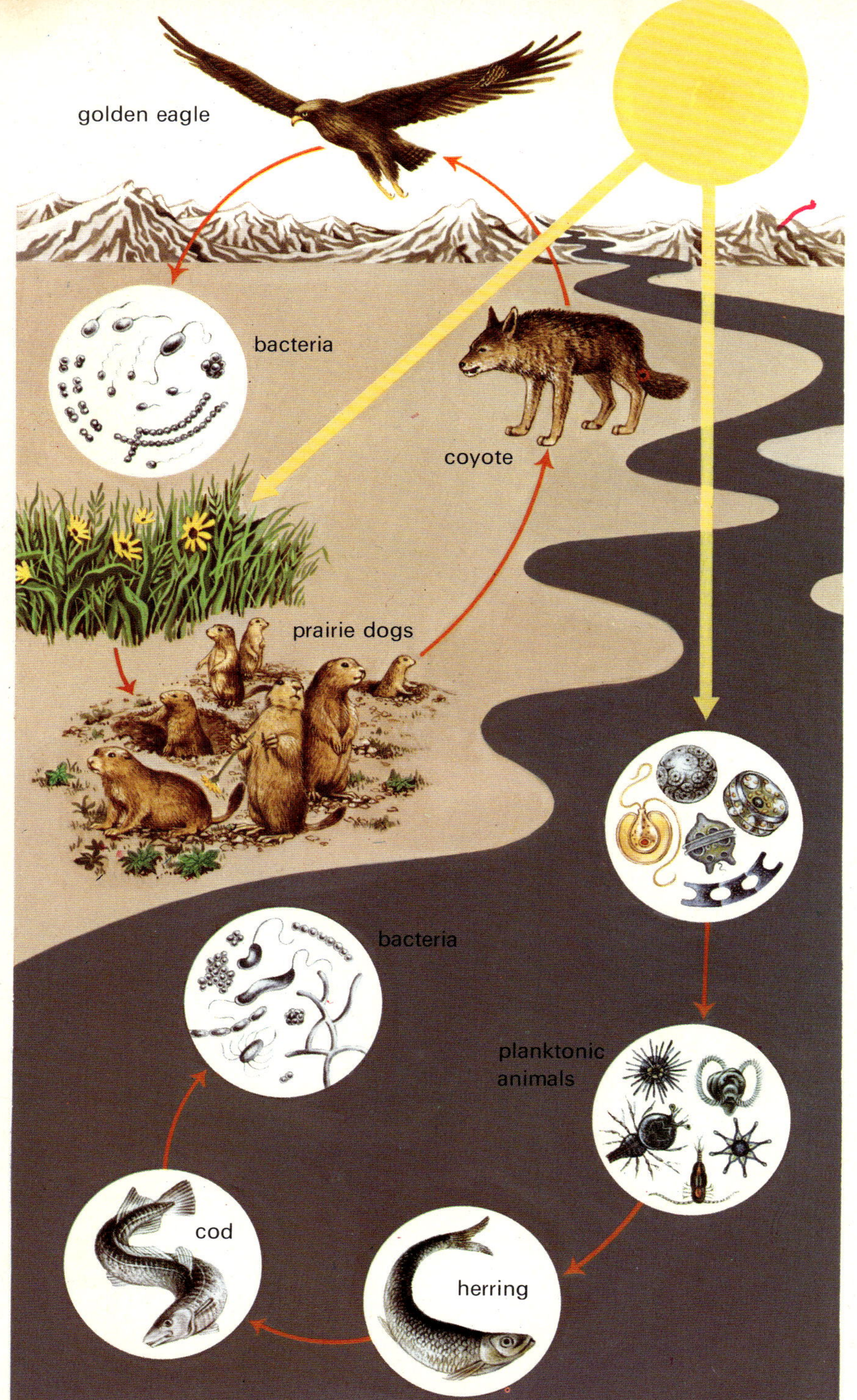

Animals at Large

No animal can live entirely alone. It must always have plants or other animals to eat, and it usually has enemies that are ready to eat it. Every animal is therefore part of a food chain, in which each thing is eaten by the one above it. The first link in a food chain is always a plant, and the next is a plant-eating animal or herbivore. Then come one or more meat-eating animals or carnivores. The last link in the chain is known as the top predator. It has no enemies.

There are many food chains in a single habitat. They are all linked together into a complex *food web*. A single tree, for example, can support and feed many different kinds of insects, and these in turn feed many kinds of birds. The birds in their turn may be eaten by cats or hawks. All of these chains are based on a single type of tree.

Each animal in a food chain is specially adapted for feeding in a particular way. Lots of different kinds or species can thus live together without competing too much. The many plant-eating antelopes and other mammals of the African savanna can live side by side because they do not eat exactly the same kinds of food.

The eat and be eaten system of nature ensures that the number of animals in a particular place stays more or less the same from year to year. If one species gets too numerous it will eat up too much of its food supply. Food will then be scarce and many of the animals will starve, bringing the population back to its normal level.

Food chains on a North American prairie, and in the sea. All animals depend on the way plants make food from the Sun's light. On land, the prairie dogs eat plants. They may be eaten by the coyote, which in turn may be the prey of the golden eagle. The eagle is a top predator – no other creature eats it – but when it dies its body will be broken down by microscopic bacteria. These produce nitrogen and other chemicals which feed plants. In the sea, the Sun's light nourishes minute plants which float about as part of the plankton. These feed planktonic animals, which form the diet of herrings. Larger fish, such as the cod, eat herrings. Just as on land, the bodies of dead fish nourish bacteria.

Zebras and antelopes quench their thirst at a waterhole on the African savanna. In the distance are more antelopes and a lone giraffe. All these plant-eaters can survive in the same habitat, because each eats different plants, or different parts of the same plant.

The animal kingdom is split up into about thirty major groups. The members of each are all built to the same basic plan. All the backboned animals, for example, belong to the group known as the Chordata. Although the skeletons, nerves, and food canals of the backboned animals are all very much alike, the animals range from tiny fishes to huge elephants and the Chordata is therefore divided into a number of classes. The backboned animals or vertebrates make up only about 45,000 of the million or so known kinds of animals. All the others are known as invertebrates and their bodies are built along several different lines. By far the largest of the invertebrate groups is the group known as the arthropods, which includes insects, crabs, and spiders.

Mammals are warm-blooded animals which feed their young on milk from the mother's body. All mammals have hair – but some, like Man, do not have very much! Mammals are the most advanced of the animals. Here a pony feeds her foal.

The invertebrates include creatures as different as spiders, butterflies, and earthworms.

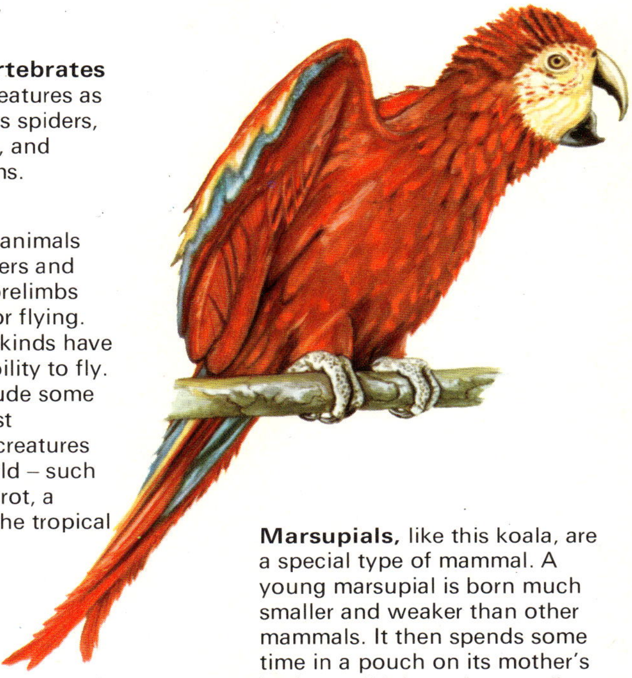

Birds are animals with feathers and wings – forelimbs adapted for flying. But some kinds have lost the ability to fly. Birds include some of the most colourful creatures in the world – such as this parrot, a native of the tropical forest.

Fish are divided into two major groups – those like the dogfish (above), with skeletons of cartilage, and those like the cod (left), with skeletons of bone.

Marsupials, like this koala, are a special type of mammal. A young marsupial is born much smaller and weaker than other mammals. It then spends some time in a pouch on its mother's body, until it is ready to walk. Once marsupials lived all over the world. But today they all live in Australasia, except for the opossums of the Americas.

Amphibians spend part of their lives in water and part as air-breathing land animals. The frog looks very different from its water-living young – the tadpole.

The reptiles include crocodiles and snakes (below). All are cold-blooded (their body temperature matches that of their surroundings) and most of them lay eggs.

Regions of the World

Animals live in almost every place on the Earth. But obviously we do not find the same animals everywhere. Each animal is adapted for life in a certain kind of surroundings – its *habitat* – and so must stay in particular areas. Many different things affect where an animal can live. Climate is the most important.

Across the globe we can recognize six major 'life zones'. These are: tropical forests, grasslands, deserts, deciduous forests, coniferous forests, and the cold polar regions. The animal life in each zone is very different from that in any of the others. Oceans and their shores provide homes for still more different kinds of animals, and so do lakes and rivers in all parts of the world. Mountains can be found in any region, but even in the hottest parts of the world their highest peaks are always very cold and windy, and special kinds of animals live there.

There are deserts, forests, and grasslands in all the continents. But the animals of an African desert, for example, are not the same as those of an American desert. They may look alike, because the conditions they are adapted for are similar. But they may not even be related. Cut off from each other by seas and mountain barriers, animals in different continents have evolved in different ways, and have produced different species.

Evolution

Evolution is a process of gradual change in plants and animals. It is through this slow change from generation to generation that the simple animals and plants of long ago gave rise to the wide variety of creatures that we see today. The same process has ensured that each kind of animal and plant is well suited to its particular habitat. In each generation there are always some individuals that are stronger or more efficient than the others. These are the ones that are most likely to survive and breed. Their offspring are also likely to be strong and efficient, and so the whole population gradually improves. Individuals that do not fit in with their surroundings are continually weeded out by their enemies. Conditions are not the same everywhere, and so something that is useful in one region may be useless in another. So animals evolve in different ways in different places, and this is how the wide variety of today's creatures has come about.

Polar regions are very cold all the year round. Animals here need to be adapted to keep warm. These seals have a layer of fat under the skin.

Deserts are places where little rain falls. Most are very hot. Desert animals must be able to keep cool, and live on very little water. The fennec fox's large ears lose heat from its body.

Tropical forests are hot and wet. There are flowers and fruit all the year round. These feed many colourful insects and birds.

Temperate forests are of two main types. Coniferous forests are found in the colder parts. Their trees do not shed leaves in winter. Deciduous trees do lose their leaves, and grow in slightly warmer places. Both types are homes for many birds, insects, and mammals, which all depend on the trees for food.

Grasslands are of many types. Some support huge herds of plant-eating animals. These American bison are found on the great prairies.

Incredible Journeys

Although most animals can live in only one region or habitat, some make incredible journeys from one region to another. These journeys are called migrations, and they usually take place at particular seasons of the year. Many birds, for example, fly north in the spring and south again in the autumn. This allows them to enjoy the northern summer, with its good supply of insect food, without having to live there in the winter cold. Birds are the best-known migrants, but many mammals, insects, and fishes also migrate to and from breeding grounds and seasonal feeding grounds. The animals do not have to be shown the way. They know which way to go by instinct, and they are guided by the sun and the stars and possibly also by the earth's magnetic field.

The cuckoo spends each winter in the warmth of Africa. It breeds in Europe. The hen cuckoo does not build her own nest – she lays her egg in another bird's nest. The new 'parents' feed the young cuckoo when it hatches. The 'parent' bird above is a reed warbler.

The monarch butterfly of North America is the champion migrator among insects. It travels 4000 kilometres from Hudson Bay in Canada to Florida, USA.

Reindeer and Caribou roam in great herds across the Arctic tundra from one feeding ground to the next.

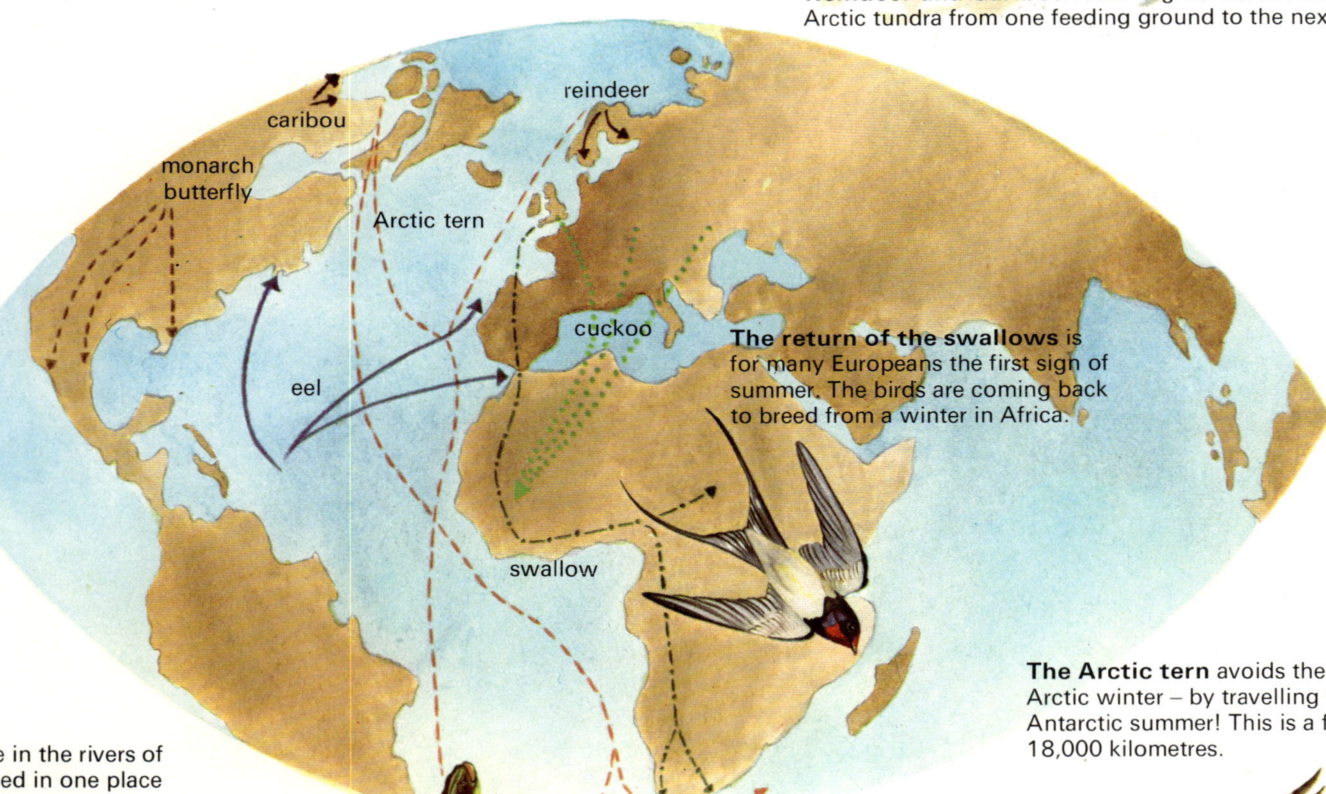

The return of the swallows is for many Europeans the first sign of summer. The birds are coming back to breed from a winter in Africa.

The Arctic tern avoids the terrible Arctic winter – by travelling to the Antarctic summer! This is a flight of 18,000 kilometres.

The eels which live in the rivers of Europe all go to breed in one place – the Sargasso Sea. This is a region of still water and dense seaweed in the middle of the Atlantic Ocean. Millions of tiny larvae hatch from the eels' eggs. These drift back to Europe with the ocean currents. The journey takes three years. They spend up to nine years in the rivers before they are ready to breed. American eels also breed in the Sargasso Sea, but their journey has not been fully studied.

Polar Lands

The **Arctic tern** migrates between the Arctic and the Antarctic.

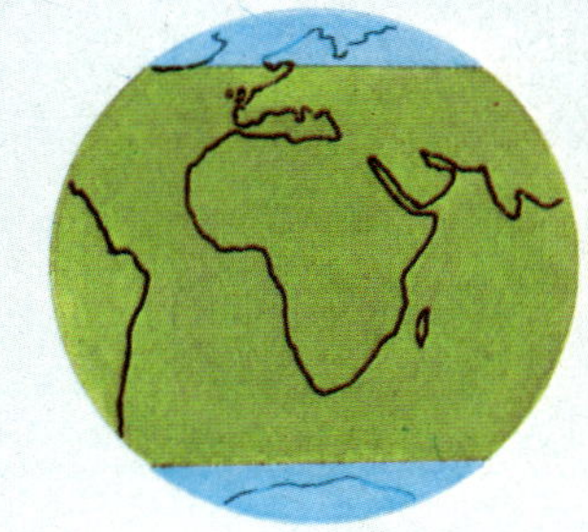

A caribou walks across the Arctic tundra. The animals on this page all live in this region of moss and scrub.

The polar regions are those areas surrounding the North and South Poles. They are very cold, with long winters and short summers. There is at least one day in the winter when the sun never rises. And right at the pole there is a six-month period of darkness during the winter. On the other hand, there is at least one day in summer when the sun never sets, and the pole itself has a six-month period of daylight. But it is still very cold.

The Arctic region extends from the North Pole down to the tree line, which is the northern edge of the coniferous forests. There is no land at the pole itself, just a vast frozen ocean. But farther south, between the tree line and the shores of the Arctic Ocean, there is the windswept tundra. This huge region is frozen for much of the year, but the ice melts for the short summer. Then the tundra becomes a blaze of colour as thousands of low-growing plants come into flower. At this time of year the tundra is home to millions of insects and birds, and also to many mammals, such as the reindeer or caribou, the arctic hare, the lemming, and the musk ox. Wolves, arctic foxes, and snowy owls feed on the plant-eating mammals. Most of the birds fly south before winter returns, and the reindeer also move south into the forests where they can find food more easily. Lemmings stay on the tundra and find enough grass and other food to eat by tunnelling along under the snow. Musk oxen stay and scrape the snow away with their hooves to get at the sparse winter grasses. Arctic hares also stay out on the tundra for the winter and, like several other animals, they turn white. This makes them difficult for enemies to see against the snow.

The **Arctic region** includes both tundra (coloured green) and ice-cap.

+ North Pole

Musk oxen live in herds on the tundra. If attacked by wolves, the herd forms a circle around the weaker members to defend them.

The snowy owl has to hunt by day and night, because of the enormous variation in the length of the day near the Pole. Most owls, of course, hunt only at night.

The Arctic hare is a large hare which turns white in winter. It lives on the tundra of Canada, Alaska, and Greenland.

The Arctic fox turns white in winter – in summer it is brown. Sometimes in winter it makes a 'refrigerator' of snow to store the bodies of lemmings.

Lemmings are small burrowing rodents with thick fur. They are the main diet of many Arctic predators.

The Arctic pack ice is a cold and savage home for a few animals. All rely on the sea for food. Here a group of walruses huddle together for warmth.

Polar bears are the largest predators of the Arctic. They are strong swimmers and eat mainly seals.

Walruses live around the coasts of the Arctic ocean, and come ashore to sleep or sunbathe in large herds. They are easily distinguished from other seals by their ivory tusks. These are used as weapons and also for digging up shellfish and making holes in the ice.

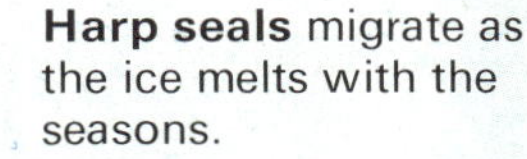

Harp seals migrate as the ice melts with the seasons.

The skua is a predatory bird, which often takes the eggs and young of penguins.

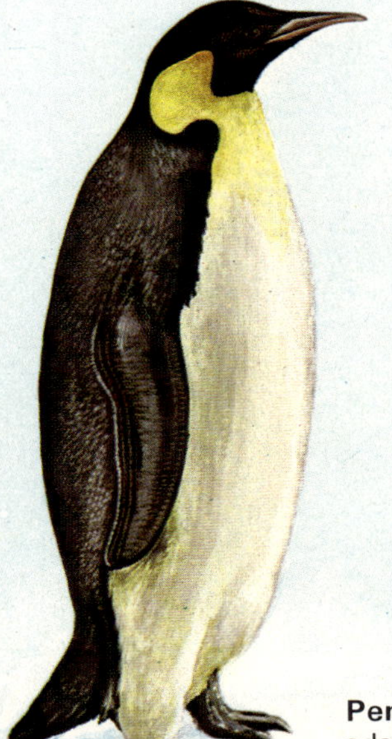

The Antarctic region surrounds the South Pole. Most of it is the vast continent of Antarctica. Apart from a narrow strip along the coast, the continent is covered with ice all through the year. A few small plants and some minute insects live on the coastal strip, but the only animal of any size that lives on the Antarctic continent all the time is a bird known as the sheathbill. It is a pigeon-like bird and it feeds by scavenging on the shore and around the penguin colonies. Emperor and Adélie penguins breed on the Antarctic continent, and so do a few other birds, but they all go off to feed at sea when the breeding season is over.

Several kinds of seals live in the seas around Antarctica, and come out on to the pack ice to breed. No mammals actually live on the continent. The seals shown here are crab-eater seals.

Penguins are birds that have completely adapted to life in the sea – except for breeding. Their wings, useless for flying, have become strong flippers.

The continent of Antarctica is almost entirely covered with ice.

The leopard seal is a strong predator. It often attacks penguins in the water.

Deserts

Deserts are areas with less than 25 centimetres of rain each year. The little rain that does fall may all arrive in the space of a few hours. Some deserts get no rain for years on end. The plants and animals that live there need to be specially adapted to survive the long drought. Some deserts are in very cold regions, but most are in the hotter parts of the world and the animals have to cope with great heat. There are few clouds, and the sun beats down fiercely all day. But at night the desert can get very cold, for the lack of clouds means that the heat can escape back into space when the sun sets. Most of the desert animals are active in the early part of the night. A surprising number of different kinds of animals manage to live in the desert by changing their behaviour. Even frogs and toads have become adapted for desert life. They lay their eggs as soon as the rains come, and the tadpoles grow amazingly quickly. They turn into little frogs or toads before the pools dry up again and they then bury themselves down in the sand where they can stay moist until the next rains come.

Deserts are not always the vast areas of sand that most people imagine. Some consist of stones and solid rock. Here a group of camels wander in the shade of a rocky cliff in the Near East. Deserts need not even be hot – the Gobi desert of Asia is one of the world's driest places, but very cold.

A rattlesnake chases a kangaroo rat – its main prey. The snake has a specially adapted loose jaw, which allows it to swallow animals wider than itself. The kangaroo rat is an American animal, but similar small jumping creatures are found in most of the world's deserts.

The jack rabbit is really a hare. It has large ears which help it to lose heat. When the grass drys up in hot weather, it can get enough moisture to live by eating cactus plants.

The Gila monster is a poisonous lizard. Its poison travels along grooves in its teeth while it is biting its victim.

The sand grouse nests a long way from water. When its young are in the nest, it will travel to a waterhole and soak its feathers with water to take back to them.

The elf owl spends the day in a hole in a cactus. This is the abandoned nest of a woodpecker. Elf owls live on spiders and insects, which have enough water in their bodies for the owl not to need to drink.

The fennec fox of Africa is another animal with large heat-losing ears. It spends much of the day in underground burrows to escape the hot sun.

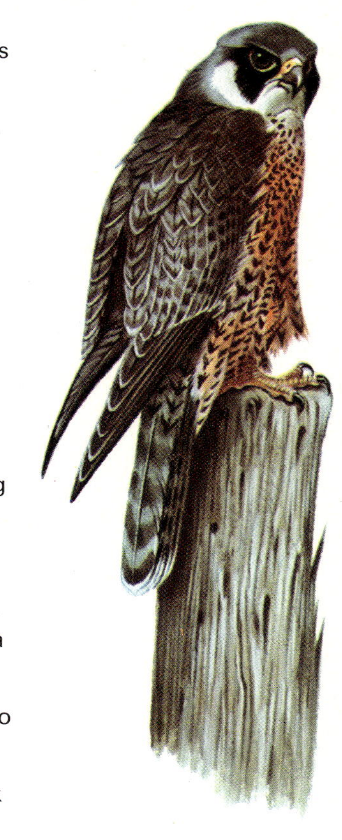

Keeping Cool

The simplest way of keeping cool in the desert is to hide away during the daytime. Just a few inches under the surface it is much cooler and moister, and this is where most of the desert animals are to be found during the day. They do not come out until the sun sets. Birds and some mammals such as the jack-rabbit simply sit in the shade of the few plants. The jack-rabbit's enormous ears lose a lot of heat and help to keep the animal cool. Some lizards lift themselves right up on their toes to keep their bodies away from the hot ground.

Conserving Water

All animal life must have water. Desert animals can survive only by using it very sparingly. Many of them never drink, but they get by on what little water there is in their food. Those that burrow down to moister levels during the day can breathe in the moist air. Sweating is the usual way for mammals to cool themselves down, but this uses up valuable water so desert animals sweat very little. Those that come out only at night do not need to sweat, but even camels and other large mammals do not sweat much. Their bodies can heat up much more than those of other animals before they become uncomfortable and start to sweat.

The peregrine falcon preys on small desert animals, and especially birds, cliffs of rocky deserts.

Camels have been used as pack animals by desert-living men since earliest times. There are two kinds, the Bactrian (two-humped) and Arabian (one-humped). The Bactrian is found wild in the Gobi desert. The Arabian is a purely domestic animal. The camel's hump is made of fat which is gradually used up to provide energy and water. This means that the camel can go for more than a week with no moisture at all.

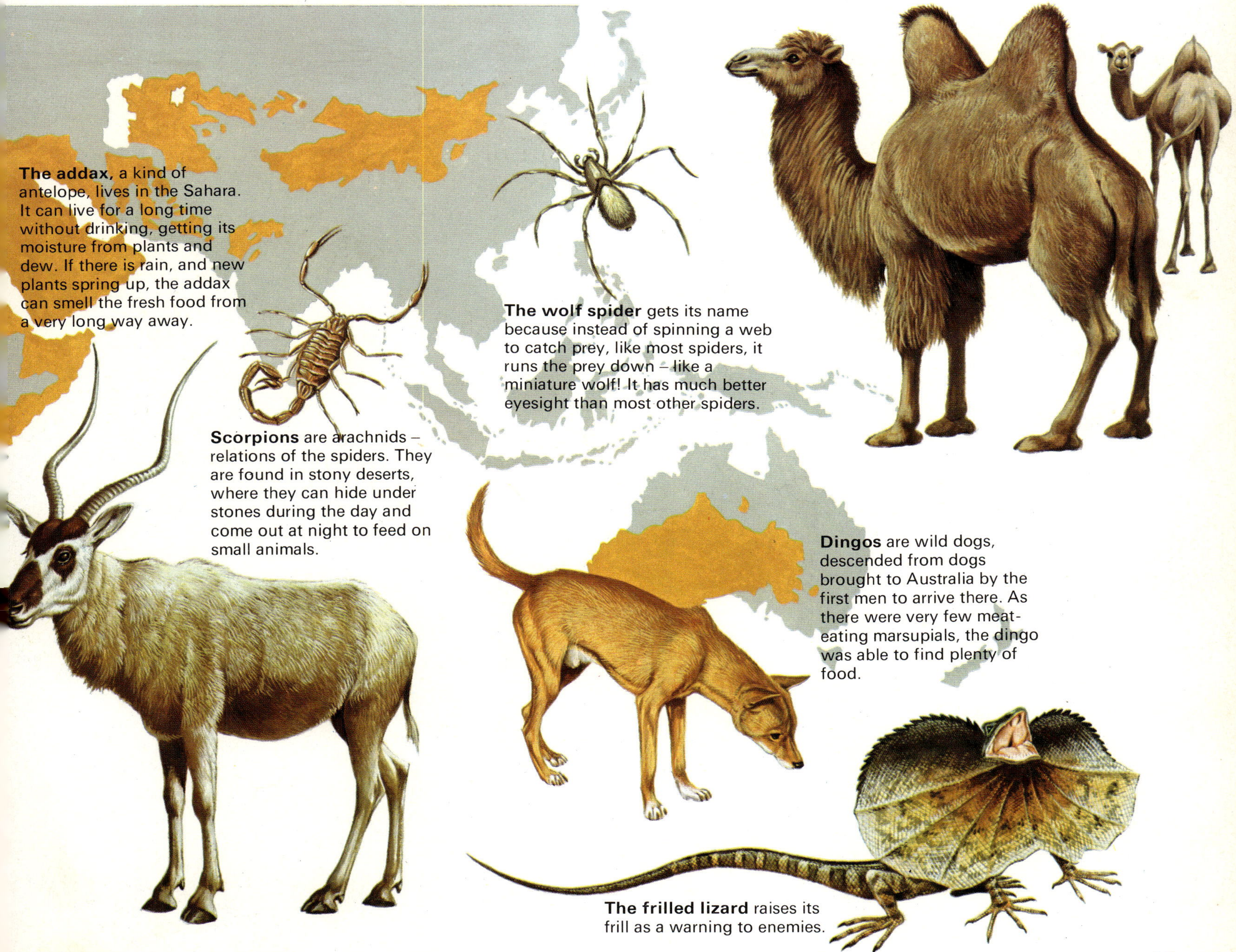

The addax, a kind of antelope, lives in the Sahara. It can live for a long time without drinking, getting its moisture from plants and dew. If there is rain, and new plants spring up, the addax can smell the fresh food from a very long way away.

The wolf spider gets its name because instead of spinning a web to catch prey, like most spiders, it runs the prey down – like a miniature wolf! It has much better eyesight than most other spiders.

Scorpions are arachnids – relations of the spiders. They are found in stony deserts, where they can hide under stones during the day and come out at night to feed on small animals.

Dingos are wild dogs, descended from dogs brought to Australia by the first men to arrive there. As there were very few meat-eating marsupials, the dingo was able to find plenty of food.

The frilled lizard raises its frill as a warning to enemies.

Tropical Forests

The Earth's tropical region – the area nearest the Equator – is always very hot, and has a very high rainfall. Here, the world's most luxuriant forests grow. These are the tropical rain forests, where plants grow all the year round and support an amazing variety of animals. The rain forest trees form a dense canopy between 15 and 30 metres from the ground. A few trees grow up through the canopy, and some grow at lower levels, but the canopy cuts off most of the light and few plants can grow on the forest floor except where light can get in around clearings and streams. Most of the forest animals live in the canopy, including many monkeys, birds, and insects. Some insects and other invertebrates feed among the decaying leaves on the forest floor, but larger ground-living animals stay at the forest's edges. Here there are low-growing plants for them to eat. The heat allows insects and other cold-blooded animals to grow to much larger sizes than they can in cooler climates.

The world's tropical forests cover parts of South America, Africa, Asia, and Australasia.

The gorilla is the largest of the apes. Most gorillas are too heavy to live in trees, so they spend their time on the ground. They live in troops, each of which is 'ruled' by an old male.

The bushbaby is an animal which is awake by night. It can see easily in the dark because of its huge eyes.

Africa

Tropical forests cover large areas of west and central Africa, from Liberia and Gabon to Uganda. They are full of animals, of which the monkeys and apes are the most famous. The gorilla is the largest of the apes. There are two kinds – the lowland gorilla, which lives near the west coast, and the mountain gorilla from the eastern part of the Congo. Chimpanzees live all over the forest region, together with many kinds of ground-living and tree-living monkeys. Several of their smaller relatives, including the bushbabies, also live in the trees. Small antelopes roam on the ground. The leopard is the main predator in the forest, but there are lots of smaller flesh-eating mammals such as the genet and linsang. All are agile climbers, often beautifully camouflaged with spots and stripes.

Hippopotamus means 'river horse' – and most of a hippo's time is spent in water. They come on land at night to feed. There are two kinds; the ordinary sort may be up to four metres long, but the rarer pygmy hippopotamus is less than half that size.

The chimpanzee is the most intelligent of the apes. They even know how to use tools, such as sticks for winkling termites from their nests. They wander the forests in bands of up to 40 members.

Many different monkeys live in Africa's forests. They eat leaves, fruit, insects, and sometimes birds' eggs. This is a Diana monkey.

The chamaeleon is a reptile which has the amazing ability to change colour to blend in with the colours around it. This helps keep it safe from enemies.

Many tree frogs live in the forests. They have special suction pads on their toes and fingers to help them cling to leaves.

The okapi is a shy creature that was first discovered in the 1800s. It is the only relation of the giraffe.

South America

The vast basin of the river Amazon, in Brazil and neighbouring countries, supports the world's greatest tropical forest. It looks much like the African rain forest, but the plants and animals belong to quite different species. There are many monkeys, for example, but they are not closely related to the African monkeys. Some of them can use their tails as extra hands, and wrap them round branches. There are no apes in South America, and no ground-living monkeys. Many strange rodents, such as the capybara and the agouti and many kinds of guinea pigs roam the forest floor. The main predator is the jaguar, and there are several smaller cats such as the ocelot. Other flesh-eating mammals include the lithe, tree-climbing kinkajous and coatis and the strange tree-living anteaters. Hundreds of kinds of brilliantly coloured birds live in the tree-tops, and there are also a lot of bats, including the infamous, blood-sucking vampire bat.

The Amazon winds through the thick forest. The dense canopy of trees cuts out much of the light lower down.

The male quetzal has perhaps the most magnificent plumage of the jungle birds.

The three-toed sloth spends most of its time hanging upside-down from a branch. Microscopic plants grow on their hair, and make it rather green.

Many hummingbirds feed on the nectar of the forest's flowers. Their wings are adapted for hovering in front of flowers.

Jaguars are very good climbers. They often stalk their prey along branches. The jaguar has long been hunted for its spotted coat and is now very rare.

The anaconda is the world's largest snake. It is one of the boa family, which do not poison their prey, but coil round them and squeeze them to death.

The toucan is a fruit-eating bird with a long bill for reaching through the thick foliage.

Marmosets are the smallest of all monkeys. They are the only monkeys with claws.

The capybara, the world's largest rodent, spends much of its time in or near water.

Caimans are relatives of crocodiles and alligators which live in the Amazon. They often catch capybaras which venture too near.

Asia

The Asiatic rain forest is centred on Malaysia and Borneo, with small patches in India and Indo-China. It is particularly famous for its insects. Huge stick insects and fantastic leaf-insects provide some of the most amazing examples of camouflage. Giant silk moths and birdwing butterflies are among the most striking of all the forest insects. Apes are represented by the orang-utan and several kinds of gibbons, all easily told apart from the monkeys because they have no tails. Several kinds of deer and wild cattle wander through the forests. They are the main food of the tiger. Leopards also live in these forests, but usually take smaller prey, such as pigs and monkeys. Large fruit-eating bats or flying foxes live in the trees, along with a multitude of birds. There are many ground-living birds in the region, too. These include the peafowl, pheasants, and the Indian jungle fowl, which is probably the ancestor of all our domestic chickens.

Tigers live in the tropical forests of Malaysia, Indonesia, and the Indian sub-continent. Some live in colder parts of Asia. They prey on deer, antelopes, and wild cattle as well as smaller animals.

Asia has rain forests which are wet all the year round (dark green), and monsoon forests (light green) which have wet and dry seasons.

The flying squirrel glides through the branches to find food. Many tree-living animals, including some frogs, can glide on flaps of skin.

The Malaysian tapir feeds on twigs and leaves. It is a relation of the rhinoceros.

Langur monkeys live in the tops of the trees. They eat only leaves.

The Indian elephant roams the forests in large family groups. It is smaller than the African. The best way to tell them apart is that the Indian has smaller ears.

The Indian porcupine is one of several kinds in Asia. Porcupines defend themselves with their sharp quills by backing towards a predator.

Three kinds of rhinoceros live in Asia – the Indian, Javan, and Sumatran. The Javan, shown here, lives in deep forest and is now very rare.

A peacock, displaying its spectacular feathers to court a female. Peafowl belong to the pheasant family.

Australasia

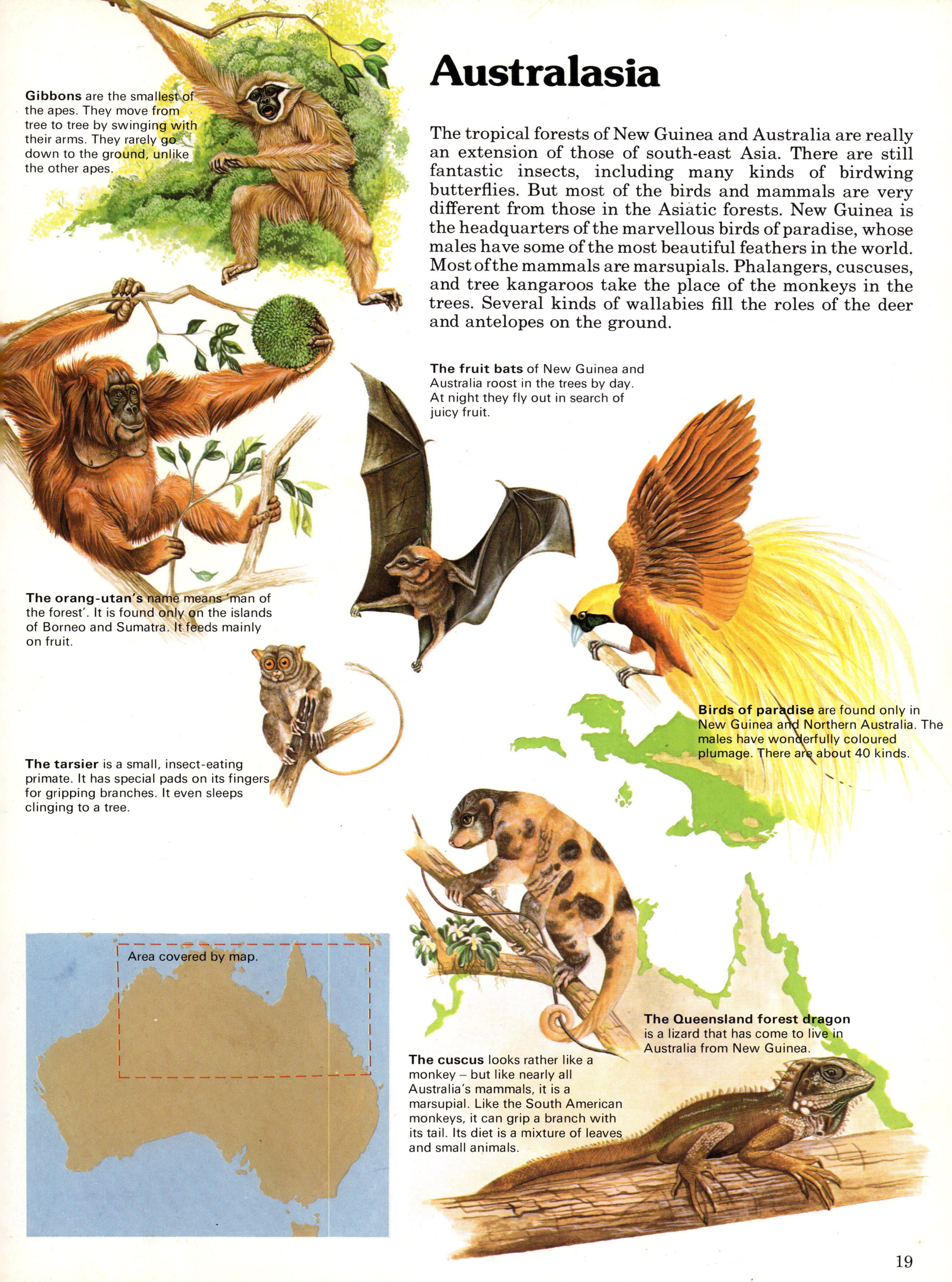

Gibbons are the smallest of the apes. They move from tree to tree by swinging with their arms. They rarely go down to the ground, unlike the other apes.

The tropical forests of New Guinea and Australia are really an extension of those of south-east Asia. There are still fantastic insects, including many kinds of birdwing butterflies. But most of the birds and mammals are very different from those in the Asiatic forests. New Guinea is the headquarters of the marvellous birds of paradise, whose males have some of the most beautiful feathers in the world. Most of the mammals are marsupials. Phalangers, cuscuses, and tree kangaroos take the place of the monkeys in the trees. Several kinds of wallabies fill the roles of the deer and antelopes on the ground.

The fruit bats of New Guinea and Australia roost in the trees by day. At night they fly out in search of juicy fruit.

The orang-utan's name means 'man of the forest'. It is found only on the islands of Borneo and Sumatra. It feeds mainly on fruit.

Birds of paradise are found only in New Guinea and Northern Australia. The males have wonderfully coloured plumage. There are about 40 kinds.

The tarsier is a small, insect-eating primate. It has special pads on its fingers for gripping branches. It even sleeps clinging to a tree.

The Queensland forest dragon is a lizard that has come to live in Australia from New Guinea.

The cuscus looks rather like a monkey – but like nearly all Australia's mammals, it is a marsupial. Like the South American monkeys, it can grip a branch with its tail. Its diet is a mixture of leaves and small animals.

"inline

The deciduous woodlands of Europe. Some areas (striped) have both coniferous and deciduous forests. This map shows the area of natural forest – but much of it has been cleared by Man over the centuries.

Animals of Europe's woods: 1 Songthrush, 2 Purple emperor butterfly, 3 Robin, 4 Bullfinch, 5 Red deer, 6 Badgers, 7 Stag beetle, 8 Red fox, 9 Wild pig, 10 Jay, 11 Hedgehog, 12 Dormouse, 13 Common toad.

Woodlands

The woodlands and forests of the temperate regions are home to a great variety of animals. But the forests are declining. Much of Eurasia and North America, once forest, is now covered with grassland – or even houses and factories. But enough woodland remains for us to be able to study its animal life.

Deciduous forest

The *deciduous* woodlands are those in which most of the trees lose their leaves for part of the year. Most of them are in the northern hemisphere. The trees lose their leaves for the winter, so they are not harmed by the cold winds. Lots of different kinds of trees make up the deciduous forests, and many other kinds of plants grow on the ground beneath them. These other plants flower mainly in the spring, before the trees spread their leaves and shade the ground too much. Huge numbers of animals live in these woodlands. Birds and squirrels feed on buds, fruits, and insects at all levels from the ground to the highest branches. Mice and voles have similar diets, but they keep mainly to the ground. Deer browse the trees and other plants and also nibble bark. All these plant-eaters are hunted by meat-eaters such as martens, foxes, and bears. Insects feed everywhere – on the flowers and leaves, among the dead leaves on the ground, and even inside the tree trunks.

The deciduous woodlands of Europe are dominated by a few kinds of trees, such as oak, beech, ash, and birch. Hazel and a few other small trees or shrubs grow below them, and many flowering plants carpet the ground. The largest plant-eating animals are the red deer, but the smaller fallow deer and roe deer are also very common. Rabbits flourish on the ground, and dormice live among the shrubs. Wolves and bears have disappeared from most regions, and the largest flesh-eaters in most places are now the fox and the badger. Both eat a variety of small animals, and the badger also eats quite a lot of fruit. The beech marten chases birds and squirrels through the trees, while the polecat catches rabbits and small rodents on the ground. Hawks and owls also catch lots of birds and small mammals, especially mice and voles. Other common birds include chaffinches and other finches, which use their stout beaks to crack seeds and nuts. Jays compete with squirrels and mice for hazelnuts. Wood-pigeons are very common, although they usually fly out to the fields to feed. Wood-peckers and warblers feed on the abundant insects. The latter include some beautiful butterflies, such as the pearl-bordered and silver-washed fritillaries and the white admiral. These are most likely to be seen around the woodland edges or in clearings.

North American Woodlands

The deciduous forests of North America contain many more kinds of trees than the European forests. Among the best-known are the tulip tree, the hickories, and the various kinds of maples which give the forests such brilliant colours in the autumn. There are also more kinds of animals in the American woodlands, but the pattern of life is much the same. The red deer, known as the wapiti in America, is again the largest of the herbivores, but the white-tailed deer is the commonest species. Squirrels scamper through the trees, chased by various kinds of martens. Deer mice live on the woodland floor. Wolves and black bears are the main flesh-eaters in some areas, but elsewhere the fox and other smaller carnivores are the major predators. They eat rodents, birds, and other small animals. The raccoon is one of the commonest of these predators. It catches fish and other water animals as well as birds and insects, and it also eats a lot of fruit and grain. The Virginia opossum is the only pouched mammal or marsupial in North America, although there are quite a few in South America. It lives in the trees and eats insects and fruit. It will also eat dead animals which it finds on the ground. The sharp-shinned hawk, closely related to the European sparrowhawk, weaves its way through the trees to snatch up chickadees and other small birds. Like the titmice of the European woodlands, the chickadees feed on insects throughout the year. They find enough during the winter by searching tree trunks for insect eggs and pupae. Many other insect-eating birds migrate south for the winter, or else they turn to buds and seeds for their winter food supplies.

Animals of the North American woods:
1 Redstart, 2 Downy woodpecker, 3 Raccoons, 4 Screech owl, 5 White-tailed deer, 6 Bluejay, 7 American robin, 8 Otter, 9 Common box turtle.

The star-nosed mole has a ring of feelers around its nose. They help it to find earthworms and other food as it burrows through the damp leaf-litter.

The Cold Forests

The osprey is a bird that eats nothing but fish. It catches them by plummeting into the water from a great height, and grasping the fish in its powerful talons.

The lynx is a member of the cat family. It is found in both Eurasia and North America.

The capercaillie is a large member of the grouse family. It eats the leaves of conifers.

The red squirrel's main food is the seeds from cones. It buries hoards of cones as a store for the winter.

The pine marten is a small and fierce predator, which catches birds and squirrels in the trees.

Chipmunks enjoy seeds and berries. They store any food they do not need at once in pouches in their cheeks.

Salmon are often found in the cold northern rivers. They travel up from the sea to breed.

Brown bears are omnivores – animals which eat both plants and meat. As well as eating honey, berries, and shoots they often catch rabbits, small deer, and fish. The bear kills the prey with a blow from its heavy forepaw.

Coniferous forests occur on mountainsides in various parts of the world, but by far the greatest of these forests is the great expanse known as the taiga, which stretches right across the northern parts of America and Eurasia. This huge forest is made up almost entirely of cone-bearing trees, such as pine, fir, spruce, and larch. The larch is a deciduous tree and drops its leaves in the autumn, but the others are all evergreens. They can withstand the harsh winter because their tough, needle-like leaves shed snow quite easily. The waxy coats of the leaves also prevent them from drying up in the cold winds. Not many flowering plants grow under the conifers in the thick layer of dead needles.

Few butterflies flit among the conifers, but there are plenty of other insects, and insect-eating birds are very common in the summer. Seed-eating birds, such as the cross-bill, remain throughout the year. The cross-bill itself has a peculiar, scissor-like beak with which it extracts seeds from the cones. Red squirrels bite through the cones to get the seeds. Many of the animals in the American forests are very similar to those in Eurasia, and some species actually occur in both areas. Alaska and Siberia are not really very far apart, and there has often been a land bridge between them in the past. This allowed some animals to cross from one region to the other. The moose, the brown bear, the wolf, and the lynx are among the species found in both areas. The American martens are also very similar to the pine marten and other species living in Eurasia.

The moose – called the elk in Europe – is the largest of all deer. It eats the plants that grow in and around forest lakes.

The wild cat is a predator of the European forests. It looks rather like a domestic tabby, but is larger, with pointed ears and a ringed, bushy tail.

Beavers are the master builders of the animal world. They are widespread in North America, and a few still live in Eurasia. Several beavers build a dam across a stream, creating a large pond. This keeps them safe from predators. Behind the dam they build homes, called 'lodges' out of sticks and mud. A lodge has a number of entrance tunnels underwater, and a single room above the water level for living. Each lodge is home for a single family.

Beavers fell trees to make their dams with their front teeth. They have strong jaw muscles, and a shelf of bone behind the teeth to prevent the wood splinters penetrating.

Strange Forests

Regions with very hot summers and mild, wet winters support forests whose trees have very tough, evergreen leaves. These leaves are able to withstand the summer drought, and most of the growth takes place during the winter. Such forests are found in the Mediterranean region, where they consist mainly of cork oaks and other evergreen oaks, and in parts of California. Plenty of insects make their homes in these woodlands, and they support lots of birds and lizards, but there are generally no large animals.

The tough-leaved eucalyptus forests of southern Australia are much richer in animal life, partly because there is more water available in the ground. The mammals are nearly all marsupials, and the most famous is the koala, which spends almost all of its life up in the gum trees. It feeds on the young shoots and leaves. Other smaller marsupials, known as phalangers or possums, also live in the eucalyptus trees and feed on insects and nectar. Many birds also feed on the nectar. There are always some trees in flower, so nectar is always available.

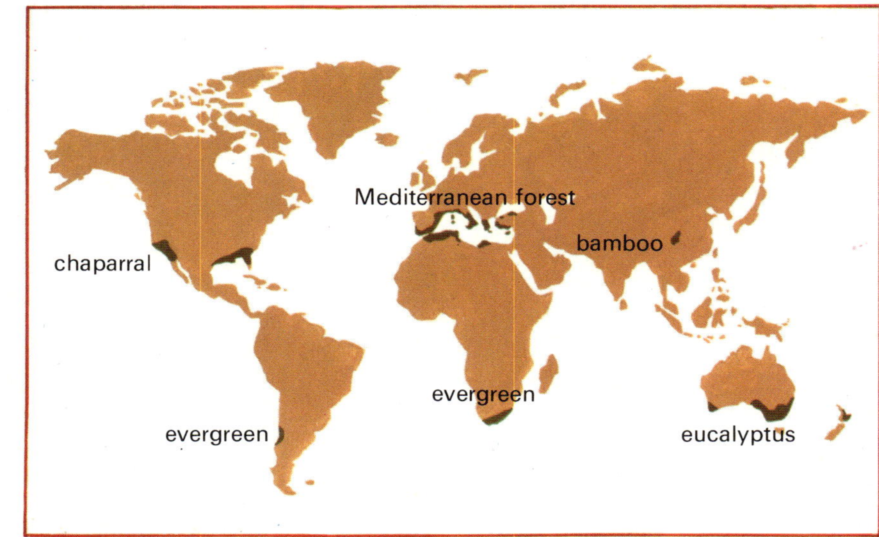

The red-legged partridge lives in the open Mediterranean forests of Spain, Italy, and France and also in Britain.

Cork oak trees in southern France. Scrub forest like this is all that remains of dense forests of evergreen oaks that once covered the shores of the Mediterranean. Man's search for timber and the grazing of sheep and goats have caused the forest to shrink and have led to much soil erosion.

The green lizard is found all over southern Europe. It feeds on insects, worms, and sometimes smaller lizards, birds, and eggs. It likes rocky places, especially if there is a stream nearby.

Forests of Bamboo

Many mountainsides in the warmer parts of the world are clothed with dense bamboo forests. The most famous, perhaps, are those of south-west China, for they support one of the best-loved of all animals – the giant panda. Rarely seen in its native home, this beautiful animal feeds mainly on bamboo shoots, but it also eats birds and small mammals and it will even dig up tasty bulbs, and flip fishes from the streams with its huge paws.

Mountain Animals

The lower slopes of mountains can support all kinds of forest habitats, but there comes a point on the higher mountains where it is too cold and windy for trees to grow. This point marks the tree line. Above it lies the alpine zone, with scattered shrubs and other low-growing plants and lots of bare rock. This zone is very windy, and even in summer it can be very cold. The animals that live here must be very hardy to withstand the cold, and they also have to cope with the thin air at high levels. Thick coats and large lungs help most of the mountain mammals to deal with these two problems. Most of these mammals are hoofed creatures, including many kinds of sheep and goats, the yak, and a group of animals known as goat-antelopes. These include the chamois of the Alps, the Rocky Mountain goat of North America, and the bulky takin of the Himalayas. The mountains of South America support the graceful vicuna, famed for its fine, silky wool. Smaller grazers on the mountains include various species of hares, some of which turn white for the winter, and the pikas of North America and the Himalayas. The pikas cut and dry grass during the summer and store it in their burrows for use during the winter. Many of the other grazers, however, move farther down the mountains for the winter so that they can get fresh food. The puma of America and the beautiful snow

A valley in the Pyrenees, the mountains on the border between France and Spain. The lower parts of the mountains are covered with coniferous forest, which suddenly stops at the tree line. Above it is the wind-swept, alpine zone.

The world's greatest mountain ranges are the Himalayas, in Asia; the Rockies, in North America; and the Andes in South America. Smaller ranges include the Alps, in Europe and the Atlas, the Ethiopian Highlands, and the Drakensberg in Africa.

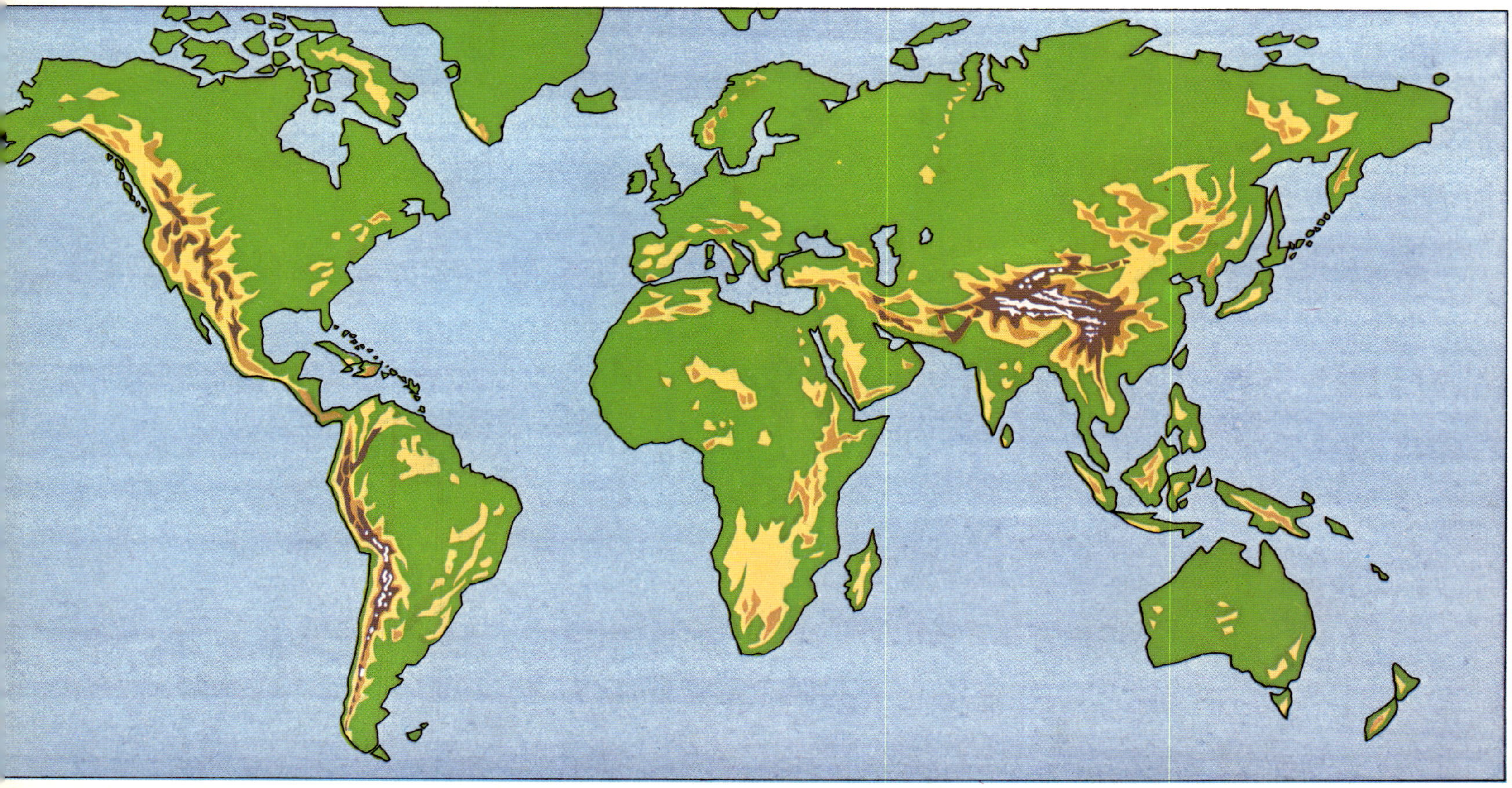

leopard of Asia both roam high into the snowy regions in search of prey, but smaller predators remain at lower levels. Only the strongest birds, such as the condors and eagles, can fly in the windy conditions. Smaller birds do exist on the mountains, but they keep very close to the ground. Mountain insects also fly very little, and many are completely flightless.

The Andean condor is one of the world's largest birds. It makes its nest on rocky ledges, and soars around the mountain peaks to look for food.

Hoofed animals, agile and sure-footed, are very common in the mountains. The mouflon is a wild sheep, now found in many parts of Europe, but originally from Sardinia and Corsica. The vicuna of the Andes is a relation of the llama, with soft, thick, silky hair. The chamois is a goat-antelope which lives just above the tree line in the mountains of Europe.

The puma, or mountain lion, is found in the Andes and the Rocky Mountains.

Pikas gather grass to dry and store in their burrows.

Grasslands of the World

Grasslands occur naturally in many parts of the world where rainfall is not sufficient to allow trees to grow but where conditions are not dry enough to produce deserts. There are also many 'artificial' grasslands, produced by the grazing of domestic animals in areas that would otherwise be woodland.

Natural grasslands are of two main types – tropical and temperate. Tropical grasslands are never cold, but there is usually a wet season and a dry season. Temperate grasslands have cold winters and warm summers, but rain can fall at any time. The grass is usually taller in the tropical grasslands, and there may be scattered trees. Grazing animals such as antelopes dominate most of the grasslands. Grasshoppers and other insects are plentiful, and so are birds. Many of the birds feed on the insects, but there are also huge flocks of seed-eating birds.

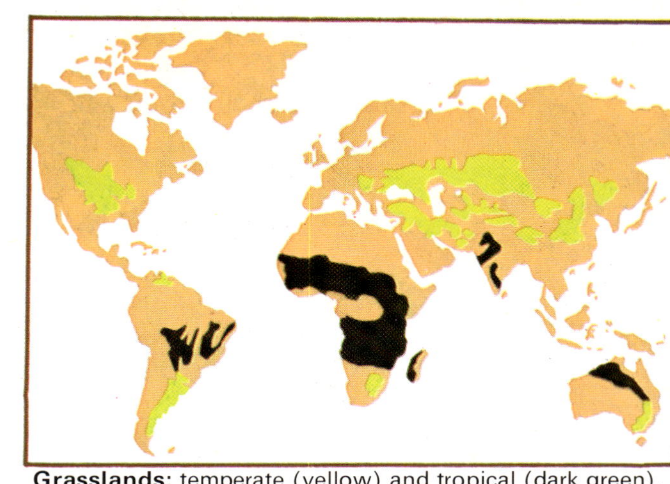

Grasslands: temperate (yellow) and tropical (dark green).

Weaver birds are related to European house-sparrows. They weave complicated nests of grasses and leaves, which hang from the branches of trees. There are often many nests in one tree.

Baboons are ground-living monkeys, which prefer the open grassy plains. They live in troops – family groups – which may number several dozen. When the troop is on the move, the younger males keep to the front, and the older, dominant males, to the back. This means that the females and young, in the centre, are protected from all sides.

African elephants are the largest animals of the savanna, and indeed the largest land animals in the world. Females and young males live together in herds – older males live separately. Elephants do a lot of damage to trees, often uprooting them in an attempt to reach the uppermost leaves.

The African Savanna

Giraffes in the savanna. The strange umbrella shape of the acacia trees behind is caused by giraffes eating their lower branches.

The tropical grassland of Africa is known as the savanna. It consists of a number of rather tall grasses and, in the moister areas, it is often dotted with acacia trees. The trees are never able to develop into forests, however – partly because the hordes of grazing animals nibble off the seedlings, and partly because fires often sweep over the grassland during the dry season. The grasses survive the fires and quickly send up new shoots from their underground roots or buried seeds.

The savanna has a wealth of big game, including the largest of all land animals – the African elephant. Giraffes roam where trees are reasonably common and eat all the leaves and branches up to a height of about five metres, giving the acacia trees an umbrella-like shape. But it is the great herds of antelopes that really dominate the savanna, although their numbers are now much smaller than they were 100 years ago. The eland is the largest species, but the most abundant is the gnu or wildebeeste. Thousands of these animals roam the East African plains, moving westwards towards the forests in the dry season and back to the open plains when the rains produce a fresh crop of grass.

The enormous number of grazing animals supports many different meat-eaters. The lion is the largest and the best known, but there are several other powerful cats, including the leopard, the cheetah, and the serval. Hyenas and hunting dogs are other common predators. Jackals and vultures come in to clear up the scraps after other meat-eaters.

Herds of hoofed planteaters are the most numerous animals of the African grasslands. Rhinoceroses, many kinds of antelopes, and zebras all roam the plains.

Zebras, with antelopes, are the main food of the lion. Usually the weakest is singled out for an attack. But sometimes a cornered zebra can drive away a lion by kicking and biting.

A lion can run at over 60 kilometres per hour, in short bursts, when hunting. It is usually the females which make the kill, but the male of a pride always eats first. Lionesses often stalk and ambush their prey as a team.

The coyote is a member of the dog family. Unlike most meat-eating animals, it is growing in numbers and extending its range. Its howling 'song' can be heard all the year round, in a chorus started by one and taken up by others in the area.

A male sage grouse displaying to attract the female. He fans out his tail feathers and puffs out a pouch in his neck. A male sage grouse has many 'wives'.

The pronghorn is a keen-sighted, speedy animal that is rather like an antelope, but has no close relations. For most of the year pronghorns live in small bands, but in winter they join together to form enormous herds.

American bison (sometimes wrongly called buffalo) are now rare outside reservations. Between July and September (the mating season) males often fight one another.

The Prairies

Until the middle of the 19th Century a large strip of central North America, from Alberta and Saskatchewan in the north to the Mexican border in the south, was a vast sea of grass. The moister eastern part of the strip supported the tall grasses of the true prairies, while the drier western part grew shorter grasses and formed the great plains. Much of this vast area is now used for growing wheat, but patches of the original grassland remain here and there. They still carry most of the original animals, although their numbers are much less. The bison, for example, nearly became extinct and is now found only in wildlife reserves. Millions of pronghorns were also shot by the early settlers, but this speedy animal is still quite plentiful in the western grasslands. It is a true American, found nowhere else and having no close relatives in any other part of the world.

The prairie dog is the best-known of the smaller mammals on the prairies. It is actually a relative of the squirrels and not a dog at all, but it got its name from its shrill barking call. It should really be called a prairie marmot. The animals live in huge underground 'towns', in which each family has its own set of tunnels. They eat large quantities of grass, but their tunnelling activities help to aerate the soil and improve its fertility. Other common herbivores include the jack-rabbit and the pocket gopher. The latter is a mole-like rodent that lives in tunnels just below the surface and rarely leaves them completely. It feeds on roots and bulbs, often pulling whole plants down into its burrows as it nibbles their bases. Snakes and hawks eat a lot of the grassland rodents, but the main predator on the prairies is the coyote, also called the prairie wolf. This is an extremely cunning hunter, often working in pairs to outwit and catch the fast-running pronghorn. But it is also quite happy to eat fruit and insects.

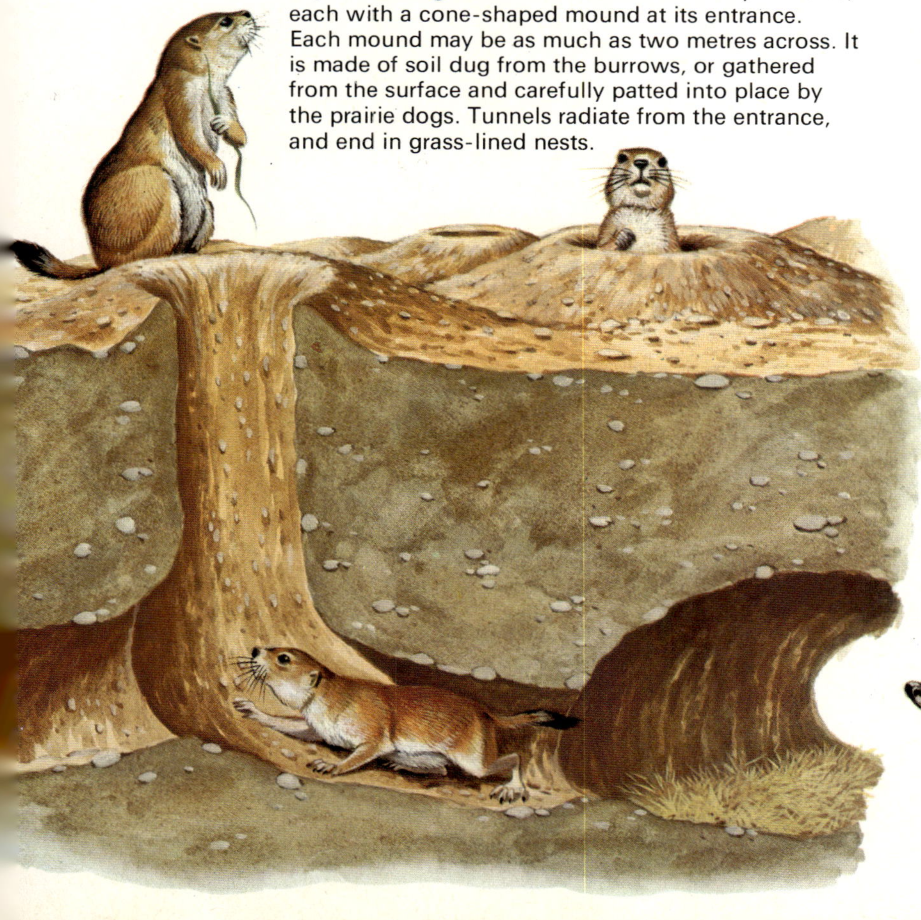

A prairie dog town is a network of family burrows, each with a cone-shaped mound at its entrance. Each mound may be as much as two metres across. It is made of soil dug from the burrows, or gathered from the surface and carefully patted into place by the prairie dogs. Tunnels radiate from the entrance, and end in grass-lined nests.

The Fall and Rise of the Bison

The bison is the largest land animal in the Americas, with males weighing as much as one tonne. It completely dominated the grasslands when the Europeans arrived there. Scientists think that there were once about 60 million of these magnificent animals. They grazed down the grasses wherever the herds moved, but their droppings made sure that the plants grew strongly again and that the prairies remained in good condition. But the bison were killed in their millions during the 19th Century, and by the year 1900 there were only two small herds living in the wild, together with a few hundred animals in captivity. Action by the governments of Canada and the United States prevented them becoming any fewer and nature reserves were set up for the animals to live in safety. There are now about 12,000 of them in North America, but there can never be many more.

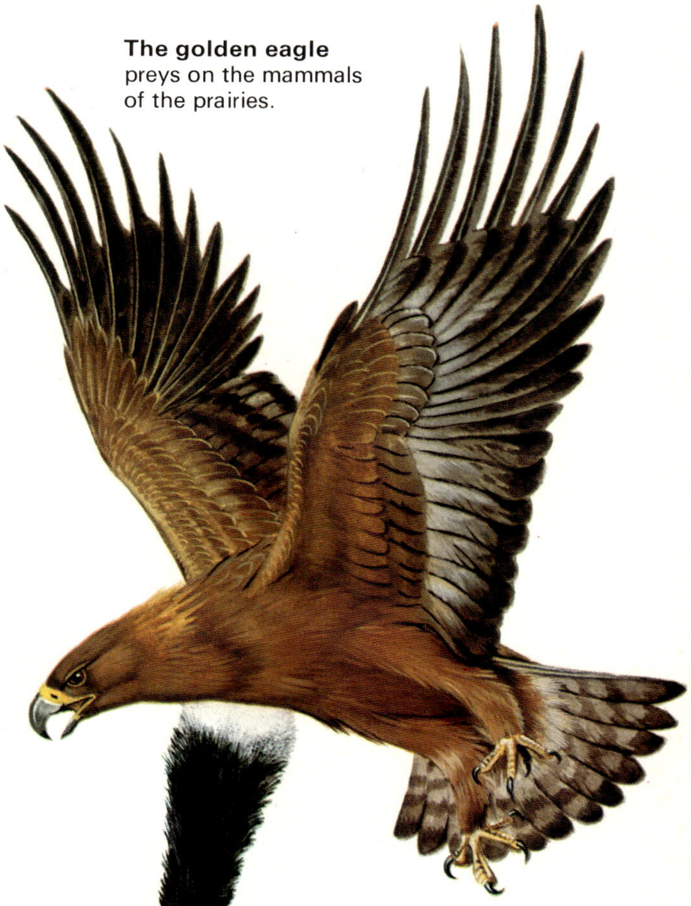

The golden eagle preys on the mammals of the prairies.

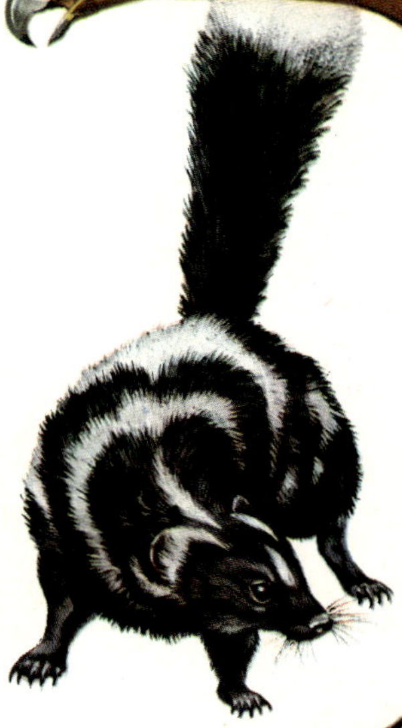

Skunks live in nearly all parts of North America. They eat insects, and sometimes small mammals and birds. When attacked, a skunk squirts a foul-smelling liquid from a gland beneath its tail.

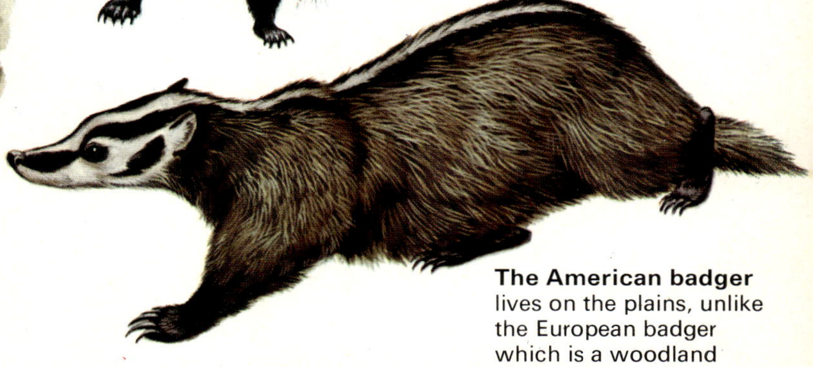

The American badger lives on the plains, unlike the European badger which is a woodland animal.

Western Europe and the Steppes

The grasslands of western Europe and the steppes of eastern Europe and central Asia are both examples of temperate grasslands, but they have very different origins. Western Europe lies in the forest zone and was once covered with trees, but man and his grazing animals gradually converted large areas into grassland. The process was helped by rabbits in many places. Much of the grassland is regularly cultivated to maintain good grasses for cattle, but there is also a lot of rough grazing on the hillsides. As well as grasses, there are lots of other flowering plants in the turf. Rabbits and hares graze on the plants, accompanied by hordes of voles which tunnel through the turf and eat roots as well as leaves. These plant-eaters are hunted by stoats and weasels, and also by the watchful kestrels hovering overhead. Grasshoppers and other insects abound on the rougher grasslands. Meadow brown and small heath butterflies, both of whose caterpillars eat grass, are very common.

Sheep have helped to form the grasslands of Western Europe. The need for pasture has led to many woodlands being cut down, and the animals' constant nibbling has prevented seedling trees from growing to maturity.

The skylark builds its nest in the grass. It is one of the few birds to sing in flight, as it hovers over the fields.

The blackbird is by nature a woodland bird. But as the woods have decreased, blackbirds have learned to live in the rougher grasslands.

Hares and rabbits are not as similar as they look. Hares, which have longer legs and ears, live on the open ground. Their young are born with furry coats and the ability to see and move about. Baby rabbits, born in the safety of a burrow, are born blind, naked, and helpless.

The slow-worm is a lizard without legs, which feeds mainly on slugs.

The steppes have always carried grassland because they do not get enough rain to support trees. Some of the grasses are quite tall and they bear beautiful feathery seed heads. The strange saiga antelope grazes over much of central Asia, while less common grazers include wild asses and the very rare Przewalski's horse – the only wild horse left in the world. Hares are common, and there are millions of voles and other rodents. Ground-living squirrels called susliks are common. There are sometimes 300 susliks per hectare. Bobak marmots are very much like North America's prairie marmots. Wolves still roam parts of the steppes in search of prey and eat anything from the saiga to grasshoppers.

The saiga (above) has a strange, bulbous snout. This holds a maze of air passages, which help to warm the chilly air before it reaches the animal's lungs.

Przewalski's horse (above), the last truly wild horse left in the world, is now very rare. The few that are left are protected, and more are being bred in zoos.

Wolves (top) are still important predators on parts of the steppes. They usually hunt in a family group or pack, of between three and twenty. Although they cannot run exceptionally fast, their stamina is great, and they can tire out and so run down almost any prey.

The steppes stretch right across eastern Europe and central Asia.

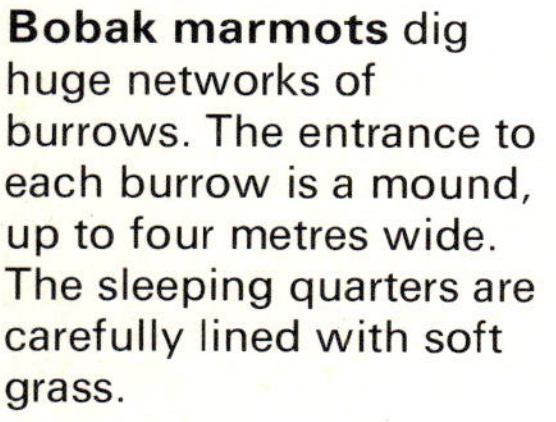

Bobak marmots dig huge networks of burrows. The entrance to each burrow is a mound, up to four metres wide. The sleeping quarters are carefully lined with soft grass.

South America

South America has both tropical and temperate grasslands. The tropical grassland, known as the campos, occurs in parts of Brazil and Venezuela, to the north of the great rain forests. Millions of termites live here and dot the plains with their mounds. Giant anteaters and various kinds of armadillo are among the many mammals living here. They feed on the termites by ripping open the mounds with their strong claws and then lapping up the teeming insects.

The temperate grasslands are the pampas. A few deer and guanaco herds graze here, but the main grazers are the rodents. South America has an enormous number of rodent species, and they live almost everywhere. The mara scampers like a hare across the plains by day, while the viscacha and the tuco-tuco come out from their burrows at night. These rodents are hunted by the maned wolf and the pampas fox, and also by birds of prey such as the burrowing owl. This and several other birds make their nests in the mounds surrounding viscacha tunnels. The birds feed on the abundant seeds and insects.

The escuerzo is a large and poisonous toad. It lies in wait for its prey – frogs, small mammals, and birds – camouflaged by its patterned skin.

Armadillos are found in the campos. Their bodies are covered with horny armour plates, arranged in bands. This is a nine-banded armadillo. When attacked, an armadillo will roll up into an armoured ball.

Many strange rodents are found on the pampas. The plains vischaca comes out of its burrow at night to feed. The tuco-tuco is another burrower, with a very loud call. The mara, with its long legs, can run at a very high speed when alarmed.

viscacha

plains guinea-pig

tuco-tuco

mara

The rhea is a large bird that has lost the ability to fly, but its long strong legs enable it to run very fast. The grasslands of the world are home to many of these running birds, such as the ostrich of Africa and the emu of Australia.

The giant anteater has a long sticky tongue, which it uses to catch ants and termites. It has huge claws for digging into the insects' mounds. It walks on its knuckles to protect these claws.

Australia

A large area of Australia is covered by grassland, much of it very dry and almost like desert. There are no deer and antelopes in Australia. Their place as major grazers is taken by the various kinds of kangaroo and wallaby. Although these animals move in a very different way from the antelopes, their faces and jaws are really rather similar, because they are all adapted to feed in a similar way. The red kangaroo lives in herds and grazes the open plains like antelopes. Smaller species, such as the rock wallabies, live in the hilly regions and take on the role of sheep and goats. The Tasmanian wolf, a large dog-like animal, was once common all over Australia and it fed on the kangaroos. It is now found only in Tasmania, it is almost extinct. Without their main enemy, the kangaroos can multiply rapidly, and large numbers are shot to make room for farmers to rear sheep on the land. The wedge-tailed eagle, which is the largest of all eagles, takes some of the smaller kangaroos and various other animals.

Seed-eating and insect-eating birds are very common on the Australian grasslands. The largest is the emu, a flightless bird which feeds largely by grazing. There are so many emus in some regions that numbers have to be controlled to make way for sheep and cattle. Most numerous, however, are the budgerigars, which roam the plains in huge flocks and eat vast quantities of grain.

The red kangaroo is the largest of all marsupials. It stands up to two metres high.

The goanna lizard lives in the more arid grassland regions.

The spiny echidna is a monotreme – that is, one of the group of mammals that lay eggs.

The rat kangaroo is one of Australia's rodent-like marsupials.

The wombat is a burrowing marsupial. Its pouch faces backwards, so that soil does not get into it and harm the young wombat.

Budgerigars are small members of the parrot family. In the wild, they live in vast flocks on the Australian grasslands.

Rabbits were brought to Australia by the early European settlers. Soon their numbers had grown so much that they were a pest. Their constant nibbling destroyed much of the grass, and turned good pasture to near-desert.

37

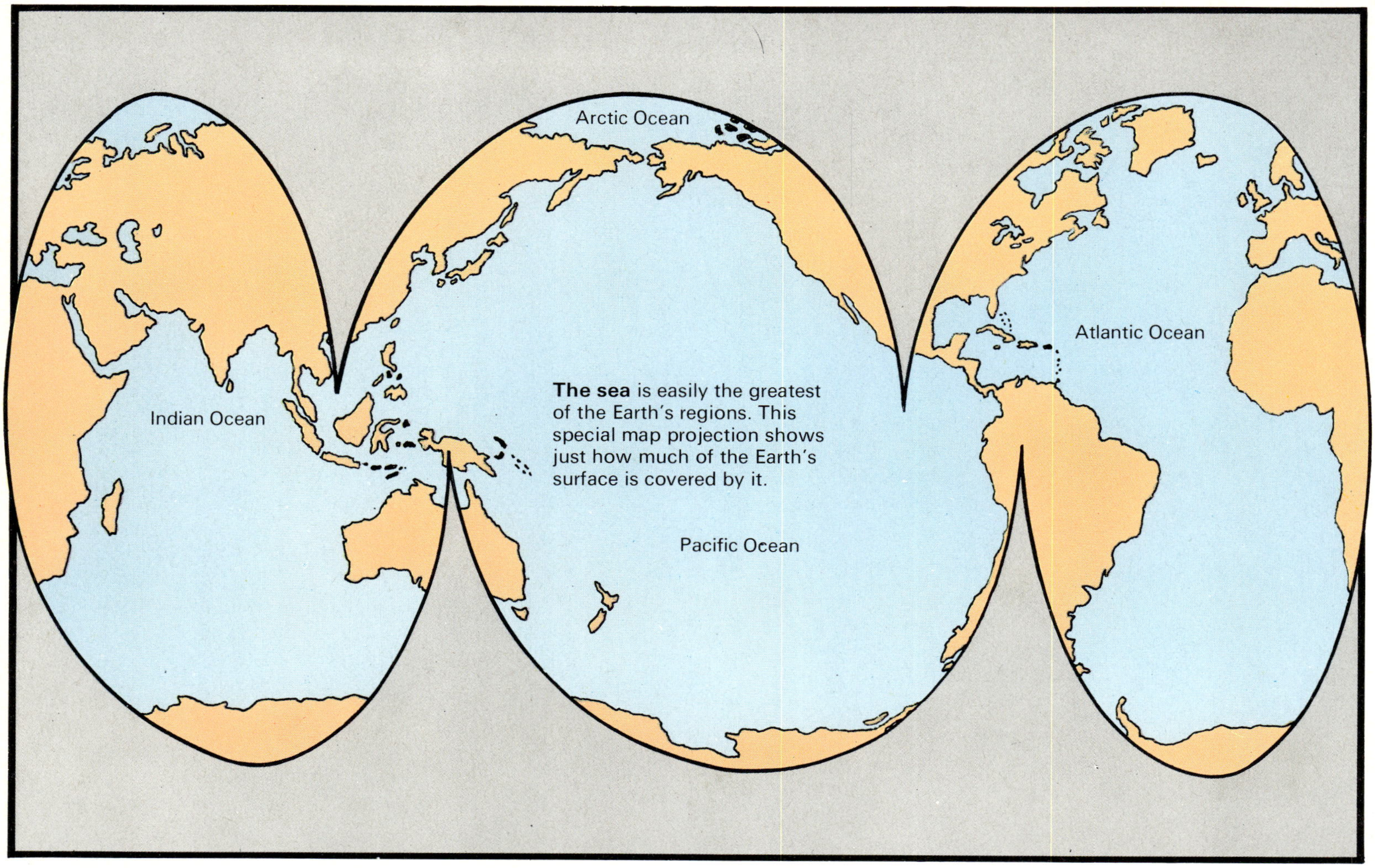

The sea is easily the greatest of the Earth's regions. This special map projection shows just how much of the Earth's surface is covered by it.

The Oceans

The seas cover almost three-quarters of the Earth's surface and contain an immense volume of water. All the major animal groups have members in the sea, and some groups, such as the starfishes, are never found anywhere else. Although most marine animals are able to move freely through the water, they do not all live in every part of the sea. Some like cold water, others prefer it warm; some like coastal areas while others prefer the open sea; and some live at the surface while others crawl on the sea bed. But nearly all the life is at the surface, for only here in the sunlit waters can the plants make the food to fuel the sea's food chains. Apart from a few floating species, seaweeds grow only in coastal areas, and most of the sea's plant life consists of untold millions of minute drifting plants. These are eaten by the millions of little animals that drift along with them – tiny shrimp-like crustaceans, jellyfishes, baby fishes, and many others. These floating plants and animals make up the plankton. The animals in the plankton are eaten by larger creatures, such as herrings, and these are then eaten by larger fishes and by the vast numbers of squids in the sea. The top predators in these chains are the large sharks and the toothed whales. Warm waters contain more different kinds of animals than the cold oceans, but the colder seas have the biggest populations. Ocean currents well up from the deep in these areas, bringing vital 'fertilizer' for the planktonic plants and allowing abundant growth.

The porcupine fish blows its body up like a balloon, so that its spines stick out, when faced with predators.

The blue whale is the largest animal that has ever lived. At up to 150 tonnes, it weighs twice as much as the biggest dinosaurs, and yet it feeds on some of the smallest creatures.

There are about 14,000 different kinds of fishes in the oceans. Between them they range from the surface waters right down into the murky depths where there is never any sunlight. The flying fishes and the huge devil fish or manta ray even fly above the waves from time to time. They swim quickly to the surface and break through to glide on their enormous fins. Herring, mackerel, and other surface-living fishes that feed on the plankton generally live in large groups or shoals. Larger fishes, such as the cod and the haddock and most of the sharks, live lower down. They swim up to the surface to feed on the shoaling fishes, or else they go down to the sea bed to munch various kinds of worms and shellfish. The plaice and other flatfishes, such as the sole, live in the plankton when they are young, but then go down to spend the rest of their lives on the sea bed. They lie on one side, and the skull becomes twisted so that both eyes are on the upper side. The skate also lives on the bottom, but it lies on its belly and is flattened from top to bottom. These bottom-living fishes do not live in very deep water, but there are fishes living out in the oceans at depths of well over 1000 metres. It is completely dark at such depths, and many of the fishes have their own 'search-lights' to find their food.

Giants of the Sea

The largest animal in the sea, in fact the largest animal that has ever lived on the Earth, is the blue whale. It can reach 30 metres in length and a weight of 150 tonnes. There are two main groups of whales – whalebone whales and toothed whales. The whalebone whales are all very large, but they feed on the small, shrimp-like animals in the plankton. Great 'curtains' of horny whale-bone hang from their jaws and strain the little animals from the water. Whalebone whales are most numerous in the cold waters, where the plankton is most abundant. Right whales, fin whales, blue whales, and humpback whales belong to this group. The toothed whales include the great sperm whale, the killer whale, and several smaller species known as dolphins. They eat squid, seals, and fishes. Toothed whales are found in all the seas. Although they look rather like fish, whales are mammals and they have to come to the surface to breathe. Fishes can breathe under water by means of their gills.

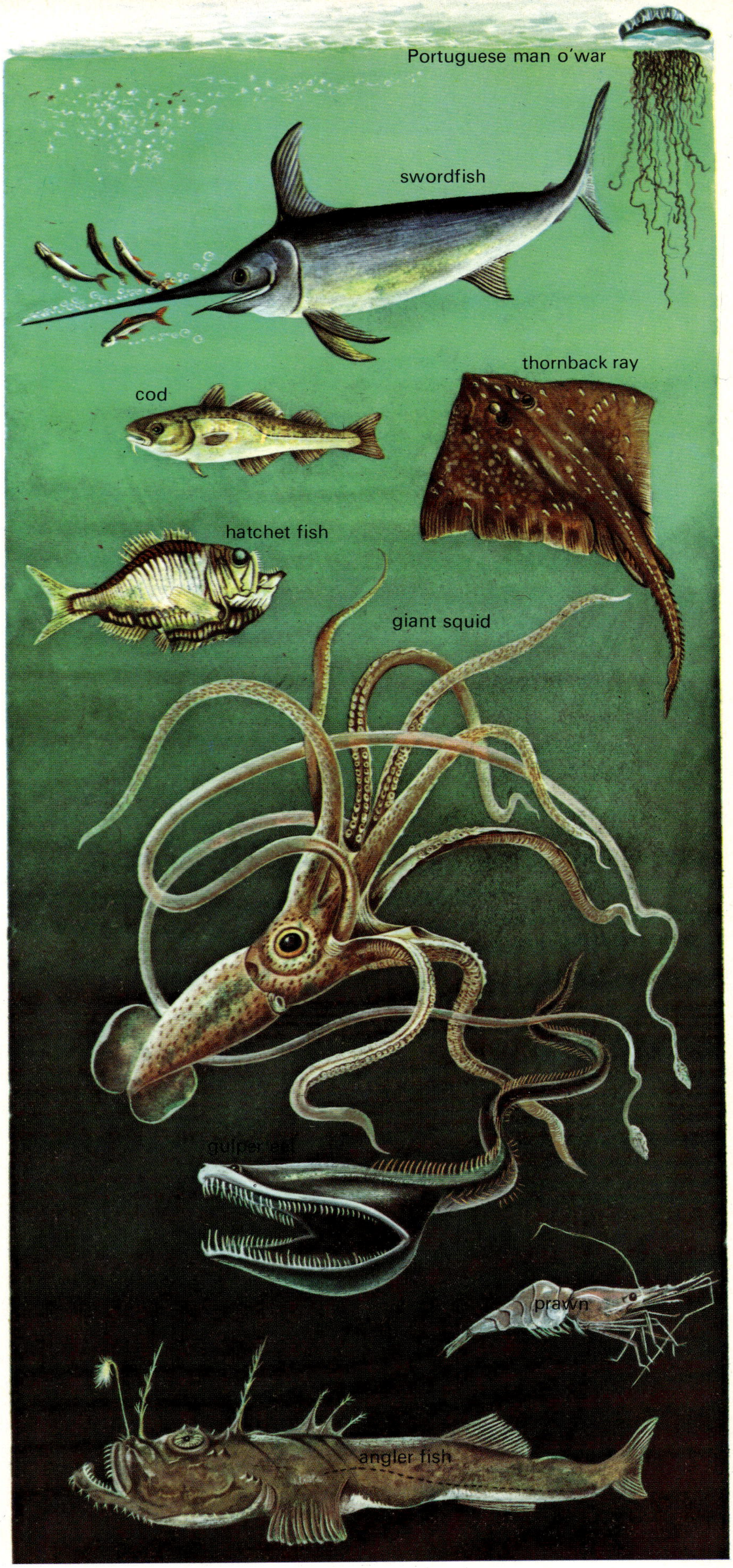

Life at different depths. The surface layer is occupied by creatures such as the Portuguese man o'war (really a colony of tiny polyps), small fish, some predatory fish such as the swordfish, and, above all, the microscopic plankton – basis of the sea's food chains. The cod, the thornback ray, the hatchet fish, and the giant squid stay mainly lower down. In the very deepest parts of the sea there is no sunlight, and very little life. The animals that do live there have extraordinary adaptations to help them find food. The gulper eel has an enormous mouth, so that if need be, it can swallow creatures larger than itself. Prawns have highly developed sense organs. The angler fish entices its prey with a glowing lure just above its mouth.

Seashore Life

Apart from the muddy areas around river mouths, the sea shores are of two main types – sandy and rocky. Sandy shores look very bare when the tide is out, but there are millions of worms and bivalve molluscs (creatures with double shells) buried under the sand, along with many shrimps, crabs, and sea urchins. These animals become active again when the tide comes in. Most of the bivalves, including the cockle and the razor shell, push their breathing tubes up to the surface of the sand and draw in a continuous current of water. They take oxygen from the water and also filter out any small food particles before pumping the water out again. The tellin has a very long siphon, which it uses like the tube of a vacuum cleaner to suck up food particles from the sand. Many of the worms also feed on minute scraps, which they filter from the water with delicate fans around their mouths. Others merely swallow the sand and digest any food material in it, just like the earthworm.

Rocky shores are usually clothed with seaweeds, and these support large numbers of limpets, winkles, and other sea snails. Barnacles and mussels are also very common. Both filter food from the water, although the barnacle is a crustacean and the mussel is a mollusc. Sea anemones cling to sheltered parts of the rocks, especially around rock pools. Prawns and small fishes also live in the pools, and hermit crabs can often be found there, living in the shells of dead whelks and winkles.

Sea anemones live anchored to the rocks on the sea bed and in pools on rocky shores. They are predators, which trap their prey with stinging tentacles.

Some of the animals of a European sea shore.
Lobsters, starfish, and jellyfish are often washed up by the tide. Hermit crabs make their homes in discarded whelk shells. The shores feed many birds. Oystercatchers use their long bills to find shellfish buried beneath the mud.

Tropical sea shores often look very similar to those in the cooler regions, although the animals on them may be very different. The sea shells, for example, are often very much larger and brighter than those found elsewhere. The muddy shores around river mouths and sheltered bays, however, are often quite different. Here are sometimes found mangrove swamps, and among the tangled roots of the mangroves live some very unusual animals. Mudskipper fishes heave themselves out of the pools at low tide and prop themselves up with their fins. If disturbed, they leap into the water and scoot across the surface like miniature hydrofoils. Millions of fiddler crabs comb the mud for food when the tide is out. The males have one normal claw and one enormous one which they wave about to attract females. Other crabs actually climb the trees and strip the bark. Many wading birds live on these muddy shores and thrive on the crabs and other creatures.

The roots of mangrove trees form a good place for mud to build up. They shelter many mud-burrowing animals such as crabs.

Spoonbills use their long flattened bills to strain the mud for minute plants and animals. They have long legs for wading in the mud and shallow water.

Mudskippers are 'fish out of water'. They have fins with 'elbows', which allow them to crawl about on the mud. Some kinds even climb trees.

The soldier crab's eyes are on stalks. It can raise them to see farther. When the tide begins to come in it makes an airtight chamber in the mud, where it stays until low tide.

A male fiddler crab has a huge claw for courting displays. Each of these crabs has a small territory around its burrow, which it will defend against intruders.

Island Animals

Islands are basically of two types: oceanic and continental. Oceanic islands spring up as a result of volcanic activity under the sea and are really huge piles of volcanic lava, often far out to sea. Examples include the Galapagos and Hawaiian Islands. They have never had any contact with the mainland. Continental islands, on the other hand, are really parts of the neighbouring continents and were once joined to them, although they may now be separated by large expanses of sea. Examples include the British Isles and Madagascar.

Oceanic islands support relatively few kinds of animals. Only those species that can survive a sea crossing can colonize an island. The further the island from land the fewer animals are likely to get there. Birds, bats, and some insects can manage it, and some reptiles and small mammals can float across on logs. Freshwater fishes and large mammals cannot manage it. Those species that do get to islands find little competition and evolve into all sorts of new forms.

The Galapagos Islands have many animals that are found nowhere else. The giant tortoises and the fifteen different kinds of finch are particularly famous. The finches on each island are differently adapted for eating cactus, insects, seeds, or other food, according to what can be found.

Seabirds form vast colonies on nearly all islands. Here an albatross feeds its chick.

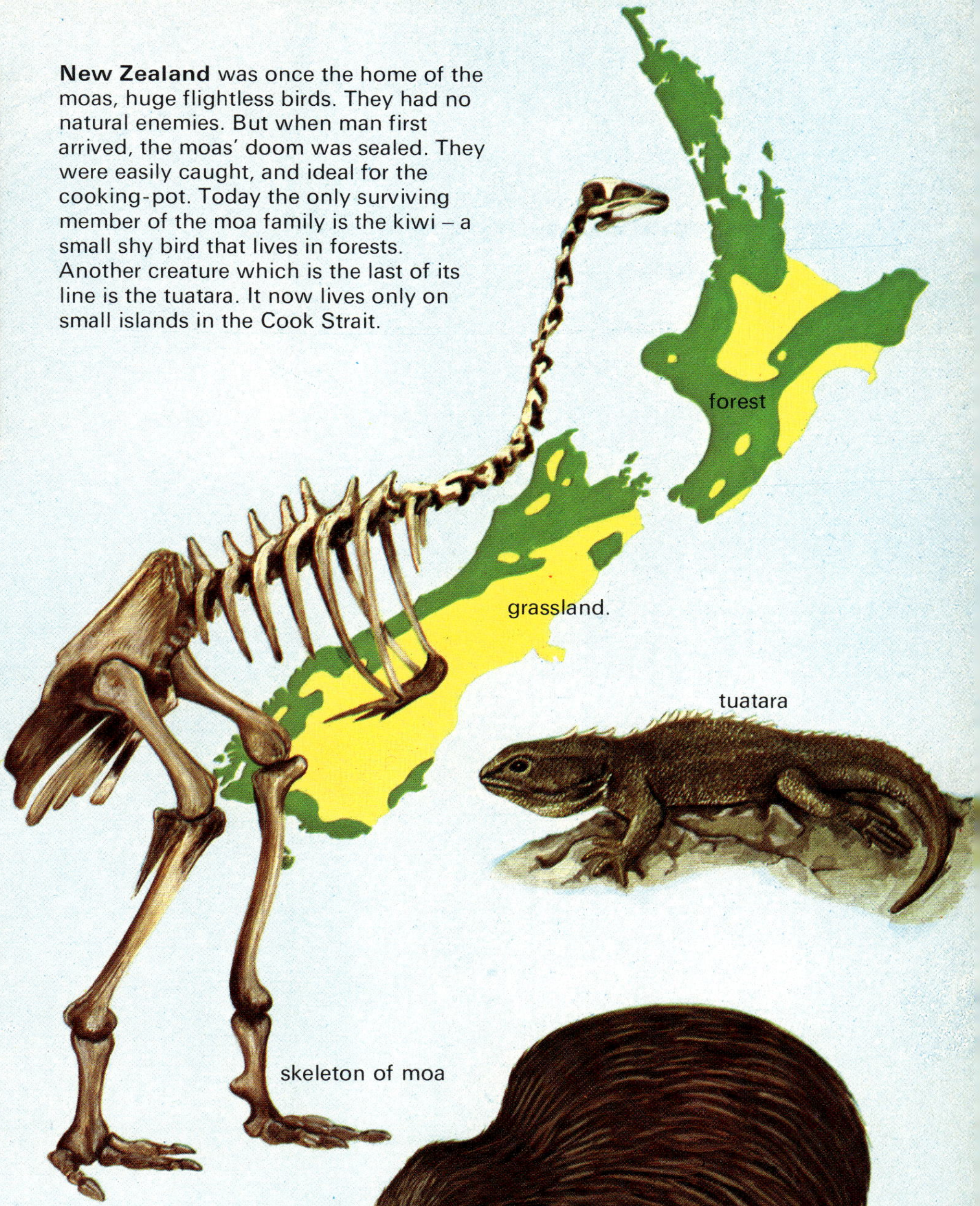

Continental islands usually have many more animals, which originally came from the neighbouring mainland. But if they have been separated for a long time their animals may be very different. Madagascar, for example, received most of its animals from Africa, but a long period of evolution on the island has meant that many new forms not known on the mainland have appeared. More than half of Madagascar's birds are found nowhere else in the world. On the other hand, some ancient groups can survive on the islands because they are free from competition from more advanced animals that evolve on the mainland. This is how the lemurs have survived on Madagascar and the marsupials in Australia.

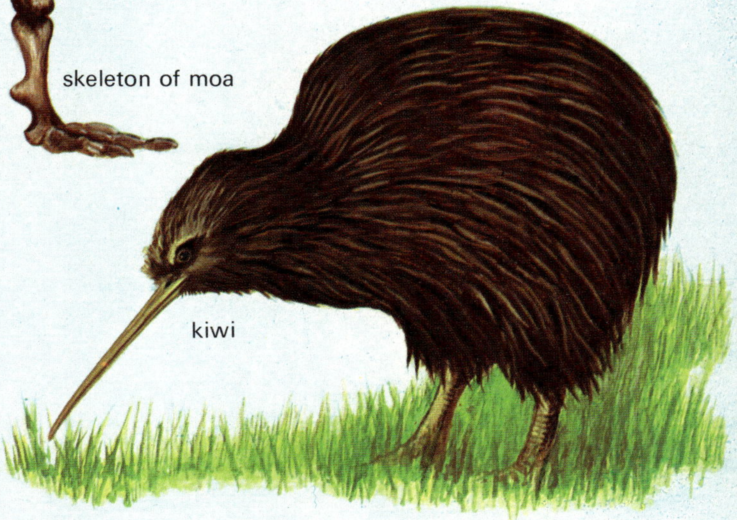

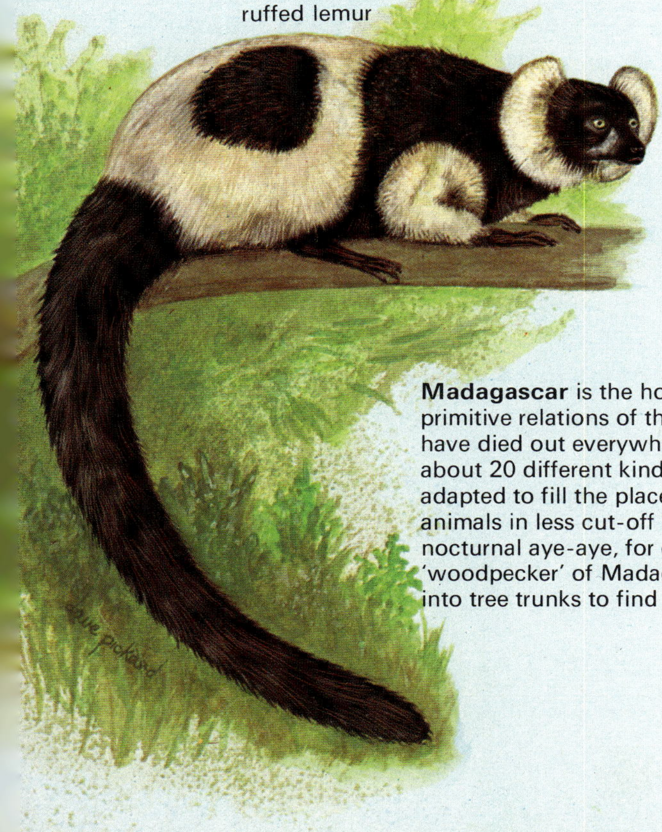

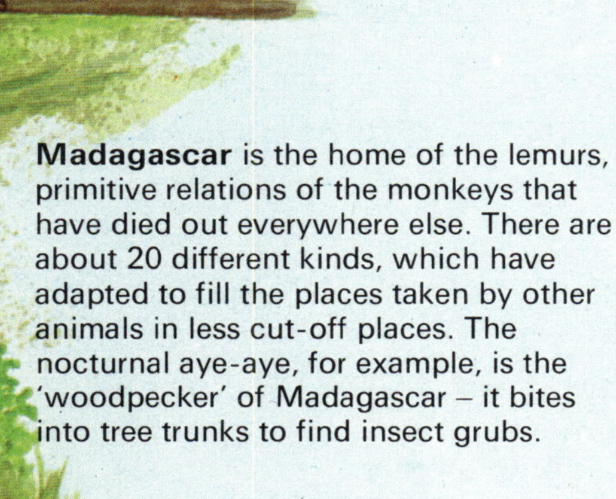

Madagascar is the home of the lemurs, primitive relations of the monkeys that have died out everywhere else. There are about 20 different kinds, which have adapted to fill the places taken by other animals in less cut-off places. The nocturnal aye-aye, for example, is the 'woodpecker' of Madagascar – it bites into tree trunks to find insect grubs.

New Zealand is really part of the main Australasian continent, but has probably never been joined to it. It is thus more like an oceanic island. Its only native land mammals are bats, and many strange flightless birds evolved to fill the habitats occupied by mammals in other parts of the world. Most of these are now very rare or extinct, largely because Man has brought in various kinds of mammals that compete with them.

Index

ACKNOWLEDGEMENTS

Photographers and picture agencies: page 8 Satour 9 Sonia Halliday (top), Australian News and Information Bureau (bottom); 12 Colin Wyatt/NHPA; 13 Seaphot; 14 Sonia Halliday; 17 David Harris; 19 P. Morris; 25 C. J. Ott/Bruce Coleman Ltd (top), R. Balharry/NHPA (bottom); 26 Michael Chinery; 28 Sonia Halliday; 30 Dave Collins; 34 Michael Chinery; 38 Christian Petron/Seaphot; 40 Heather Angel; 41 Ken Merrylees; 42 Heather Angel; 43 R. I. Lewis-Smith.

Picture research: Jackie Cookson